The MAILBOX®
The Education Center®

P9-BVH-961

grades 1

Organize SEPTEMBER Now!™

Everything You Need for a Successful September

Monthly Organizing Tools
Manage your time, classroom, and students with monthly organizational tools.

Essential Skills Practice
Practice essential skills this month with engaging activities and reproducibles.

September in the Classroom
Carry your monthly themes into every corner of the classroom.

Ready-to-Go Learning Centers and Skills Practice
Bring September to life right now!

Managing Editor: Sharon Murphy

Editorial Team: Becky S. Andrews, Kimberley Bruck, Karen P. Shelton, Diane Badden, Thad H. McLaurin, Kimberly Brugger-Murphy, Cindy K. Daoust, Gerri Primak, Leanne Stratton, Karen A. Brudnak, Sarah Hamblet, Hope Rodgers, Dorothy C. McKinney, Randi Austin, Janet Boyce, Rebecca Brudwick, Lisa Buchholz, Stacie Stone Davis, Margaret Elliott, Heather E. Graley, Angie Kutzer, Beth Marquardt

Production Team: Lisa K. Pitts, Pam Crane, Rebecca Saunders, Jennifer Tipton Cappoen, Chris Curry, Sarah Foreman, Theresa Lewis Goode, Clint Moore, Greg D. Rieves, Barry Slate, Donna K. Teal, Zane Williard, Tazmen Carlisle, Amy Kirtley-Hill, Cathy Edwards Simrell, Lynette Dickerson, Mark Rainey, Angela Kamstra, Sheila Krill

www.themailbox.com

©2006 The Mailbox®
All rights reserved.
ISBN10 #1-56234-668-7 • ISBN13 #978-156234-668-3

Manufactured in the United States
10 9 8 7 6 5 4 3

Table of Contents

Monthly Organizing Tools

A collection of reproducible forms, notes, and other timesavers and organizational tools just for September.

Essential Skills Practice

Fun, skill-building activities and reproducibles that combine the skills your students must learn with favorite September themes.

September in the Classroom

In a hurry to find a specific type of September activity? It's right here!

Ready-to-Go Learning Centers and Skills Practice

Two center activities you can tear out and use almost instantly! Plus a collection of additional reproducible skill builders!

Skills Grid

Literacy	Back-to-School	Open House	Apples	Grandparents	Centers	Circle Time & Games	Time Fillers	Writing Ideas & Prompts	Learning Center: Cool Counters	Learning Center: Gus Got on the Bus!	Ready-to-Go Skills Practice
letter identification			36								
matching letters	25										
beginning sounds			37								
letter-sound association	18										
initial consonants: *b, h, s, t*			45								
initial consonant: *f*											91
initial consonants: *l, m, s*											92
names					58						
name identification			38			63	68				
comparing names	28										
write own name	19										
rhyming										82, 89	90
rhyming words					59						
word parts	26										
color words	27										
sentence completion	21										
writing a sentence								71			
writing a question		32									
writing	24	30		46							
journal prompts								70			
creative writing								70, 71			
communication skills		32									
left-to-right progression			39								
reading motivation	22										
Listening & Speaking											
make introductions	18										
recall experiences and share orally	20										
Math											
count to five			44								
one-to-one correspondence											94
recognize and order numbers 1–10						62					
number order to 10	29										
number words *one* through *five*									81		
number words *one* through *six*											93
number words *one* through *ten*			38								
comparing sets					48						
numerals and sets			37		58						
matching sets to numerals and number words									74		
sums to 5											96
sums to 12					59						
graphing		31		46							
sorting	19										
sort by size or color			36								
patterns						63					95
Science											
names of the seasons			39								
Social & Emotional Development											
develop friendships	20						69				
self-esteem						62	69				

Medallion

Program with a digital time. Tape to a student's clothing or glue to a child-size construction paper watchband and tape the ends together.

Brag Tag

Use a child's words to finish the sentence starter.

Hooray for Me!

Today I

WOW!

©The Mailbox® • September Monthly Organizers • TEC60975

Award

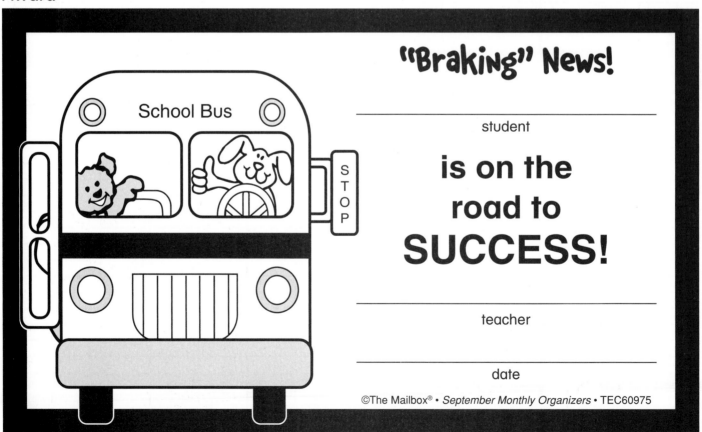

School Bus

STOP

"Braking" News!

_____
student

is on the
road to
SUCCESS!

_____
teacher

_____
date

©The Mailbox® • September Monthly Organizers • TEC60975

Medallion, brag tag, and award: Copy onto colorful construction paper, cut out, and use as desired.

School

TEC60975

TEC60975

TEC60975

TEC60975

3

TEC60975

TEC60975

©The Mailbox® • *September Monthly Organizers* • TEC60975

Clip art: Use the artwork on student papers and on correspondence such as
announcements, forms, and parent notes.

September

Sunday	Monday	Tuesday	Wednesday	Thursday	Friday	Saturday

Center Checklist

Name

Class List

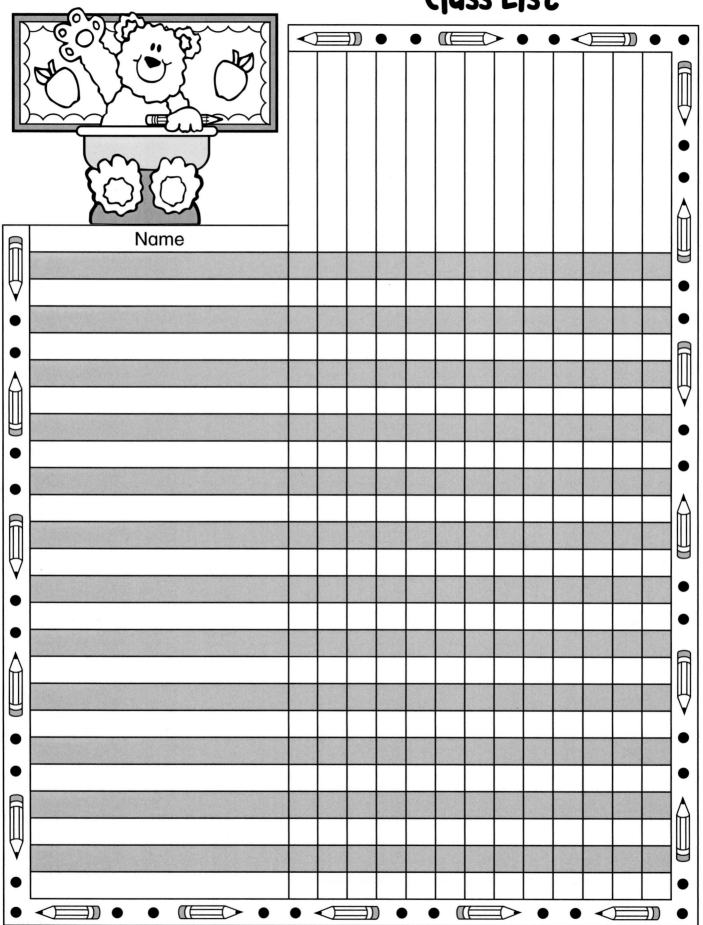

Name									

Classroom News

From _____

Date _____

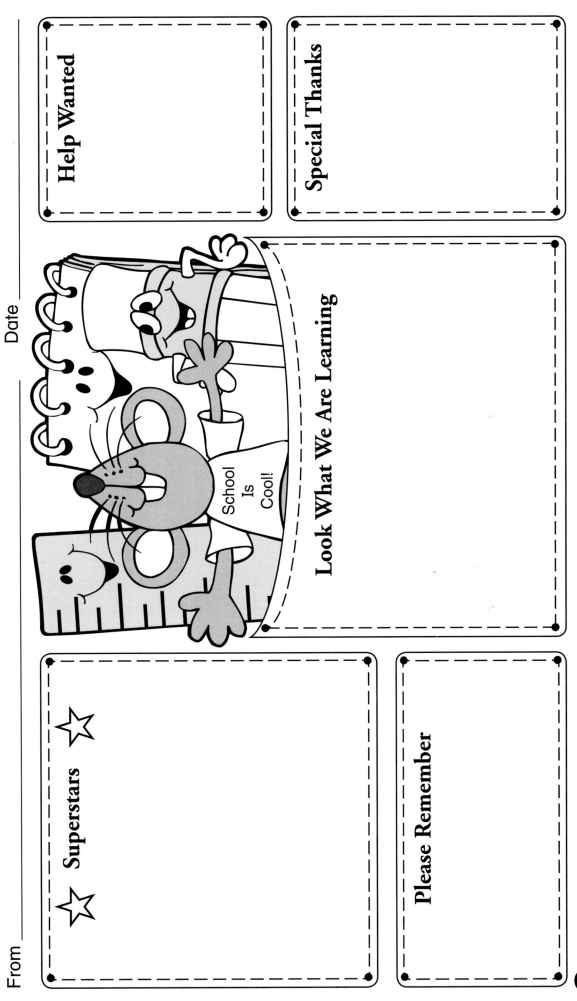

Help Wanted

Special Thanks

☆ **Superstars** ☆

Look What We Are Learning

School Is Cool!

Please Remember

Classroom News

School Is Cool!

From _____

Date _____

Name _____

Goal _____

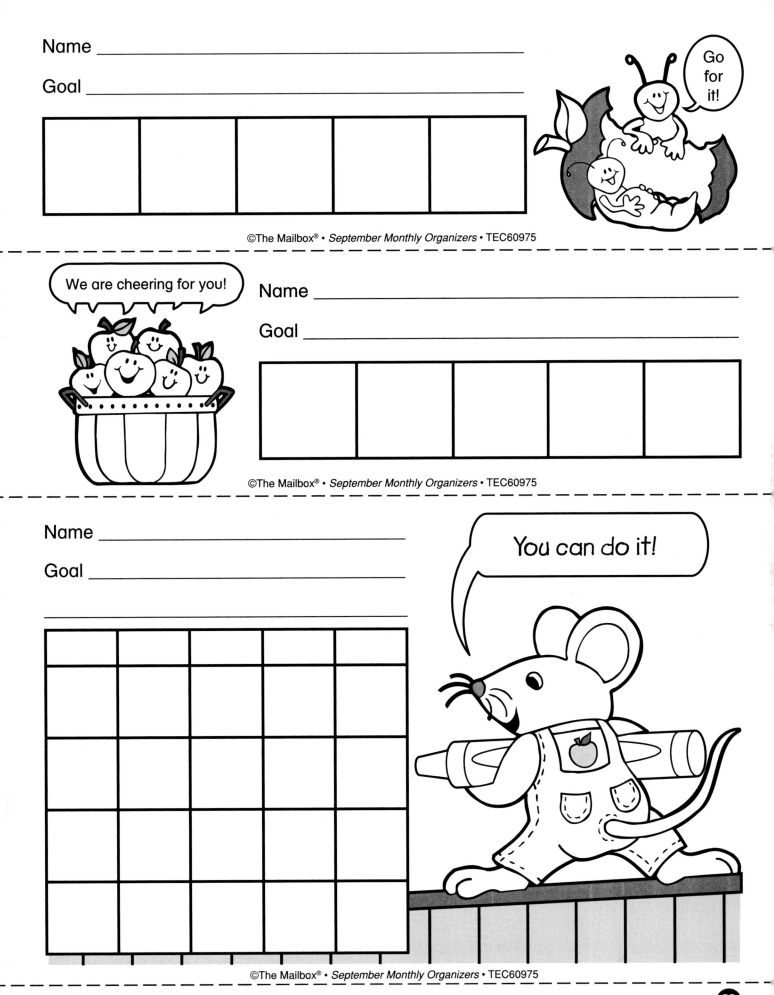

Go for it!

©The Mailbox® • September Monthly Organizers • TEC60975

We are cheering for you!

Name _____

Goal _____

©The Mailbox® • September Monthly Organizers • TEC60975

Name _____

Goal _____

_____

You can do it!

©The Mailbox® • September Monthly Organizers • TEC60975

Incentive charts: Have students track their progress as they work toward a variety of goals.

Monthly Organizing Tools **11**

My
Journal

Name_____

Journal cover: Make this page the front cover of your students' writing journals.

Materials to Collect:

Duties This Month:

Meetings:

Birthdays & Special Dates:

Themes:

To Do:

©The Mailbox® • September Monthly Organizers • TEC60975

Monthly planning form: Use this handy form to stay on top of each month's school-related responsibilities.

©The Mailbox® • *September Monthly Organizers* • TEC60975

Open: Use this page for parent correspondence and use it with students too. For example, ask each child to write (or dictate for you to write) a sentence that tells the kind of pie the cat baked or have her color (and label) two items that rhyme with *cat*.

date

Dear Parent,

Please remember

Thank you!

Parent reminder note: Use this note to remind parents of supply requests, field trips, and special events such as a classroom party, a school program, or a guest speaker.

School Note

SCHOOL NOTE

School notes: Use these notes for parent communications such as announcing an upcoming event, requesting supplies or volunteers, and writing messages of praise.

★ Family Fun ★

It's time to shine! Help your child think of several ways he or she is special. Next, ask your child to choose three for you to write below. Then cut out the shape and work together to glue sun rays around it. Use whatever supplies you have on hand, such as scraps of paper, foil, gift wrap, or fabric. Encourage your child to think creatively!

We hope to see your project by _____.

Sincerely,

_____

Glue rays around this outer edge.

_____ shines in many ways. Here are three!

1.

2.

3.

Glue rays around this outer edge.

Wow!

Learning Links: self-awareness

©The Mailbox® • September Monthly Organizers • TEC60975

Note to the teacher: Date and sign a copy of the page. Make student copies on yellow construction paper; then write each child's name on a sun before sending it home with him. When a child returns his project, help him share it with the class. Then post the project on a display titled "We Shine in Many, Many Ways!"

Back-to-School

Listening & Speaking

Make introductions

My name is Sarah and I took swimming lessons this summer.

Meet and Greet

This activity puts a spin on first-day introductions! Divide students into two equal groups. (Plan to participate if there is an odd number of students.) One group stands in an inner circle, facing outward. The other group stands in an outer circle with each person facing a partner from the inner circle. Each student in a twosome shares her name and a fact about herself, such as an interest or something she did during the summer. At your signal, members of the inner circle take one step to the right, and the new pairs share information. Continue for a desired number of rotations.

Literacy

Letter-sound association

What a Classroom!

Acquaint students with their new classroom by using this simple game. On the board, write a letter for each area of the room (or object in the room) that you would like youngsters to become familiar with. For example, write an *r* for the reading center, a *b* for the block area, and a *p* for the painting area. To play, walk to one of the chosen areas (or objects), say its name, and explain its importance to your youngsters. Repeat the name and then ask a volunteer to point to its beginning letter on the board. When the correct letter has been identified, invite the child to erase the letter. Continue in this manner until all the letters have been erased.

r b p s m a

This is the painting area.

Use the ideas in this collection to help youngsters get a great start on a year full of skills, friendship, and fun!

Write own name • • • • • • • • • • • • • • • • • • **Literacy**

Sign Time

This idea results in a handy reference for classmates' names. Have each child write his name on a colorful sheet of construction paper and place it on his desk with a marker or crayon. Designate a traffic pattern to show students how to move from desk to desk. Then, on your signal, have each student move to the next child's desk and sign her paper. Continue in this manner until every child signs each paper. (For younger students, have each child sign only the papers at his table instead of the entire class.) When students return to their desks, have each child fold his paper in half and label the outside "My New Classmates."

Math • **Sorting**

All Sorts of Learning

Give sorting a personal touch with this idea. First, ask several youngsters to place their bookbags in a pile. Have students form a circle around the pile. Lead students in a discussion about how the bags are alike and different. Decide on an attribute the bags may share and enlist students' help in sorting the bags by that characteristic. (For example, sort the bags by those that have black straps and those that do not have black straps.) Then have youngsters suggest another sorting rule and sort the bags again.

Social & Emotional Development

Building Friendship

Pair students and take a photo of each twosome, inviting them to wear plastic construction hats if desired. Have students in each pair talk to find out about their similarities and differences. Then give each duo a copy of "Building Friendship" at the top of page 23. Instruct the pair to work together to complete the form. (Have younger students dictate as you write their responses.) Encourage each pair to share its findings with the class. Then post the photos and forms on a bulletin board titled "Building Friendship."

Recall experiences and share orally

Listening & Speaking

Learning Lists

Remind your students about what they have studied throughout the school year by creating learning lists. At the end of every week (or month), have students brainstorm a list of the activities that were completed during that time frame. Record their responses on a chart and add seasonal artwork to it before displaying it on a classroom wall. Also send each child home with a copy of each list. As the year draws to a close, your class will have a wonderful reminder of all the learning that took place!

In September We...
• played back-to-school bingo
• wrote letters to our grandparents
• celebrated Johnny Appleseed's birthday by making applesauce
• visited a farm

Meet the Staff

To prepare this game, take a photograph of each staff member whom students will be in contact with during the school day. Also take a photo of the area where the staff member works. Glue the snapshots on individual cards. Beneath each staff member's photo, write that person's name and job title. Then shuffle the cards and label the back of each one with a different number. Arrange the cards in a pocket chart with the numbers facing out.

To play, a student names two numbers and then turns over the corresponding cards. If the photos show a staff member and her work area, it's a match, and the cards are placed in a pocket facing forward. If the staff member and area do not match, the cards are returned to the chart number side out. Play continues until all the cards have been matched.

Literacy • • • • • • • • • • • • • • • • • *Sentence completion*

Eek! A Mouse!

Who would want to see a mouse at school? Your students will after hearing the comical tale *If You Take a Mouse to School* by Laura Numeroff. Gather the materials below and then use the directions to guide each child to make a mouse of her own. Also help each child complete a copy of the sentence at the bottom of page 23. Glue each sentence to a slightly larger sheet of construction paper. Then post each mouse with its sentence for all to see.

Gabby says, "If you take a mouse to the mall, he'll ask you for a new pair of shoes!"

Materials for one mouse:
6" x 9" brown construction paper (head)
two 4" brown construction paper squares (ears)
six ½" x 5" black construction paper strips (whiskers)
pink construction paper scraps
2 paper reinforcers (eyes)
scissors
glue

Directions:
1. Use scissors to round the corners of the head.
2. Round the corners of the ears. Glue the ears to the head.
3. Cut three circles from the pink paper. Glue one circle inside each ear and glue the third circle to the head for a nose.
4. Glue three whiskers on each side of the nose.
5. Attach the eyes.

Management

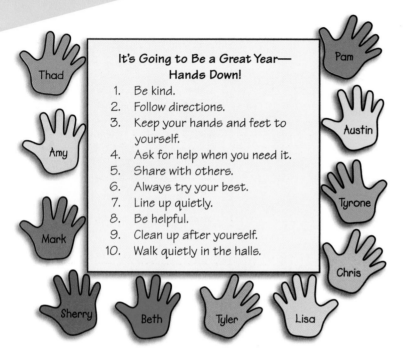

It's Going to Be a Great Year—
Hands Down!

1. Be kind.
2. Follow directions.
3. Keep your hands and feet to yourself.
4. Ask for help when you need it.
5. Share with others.
6. Always try your best.
7. Line up quietly.
8. Be helpful.
9. Clean up after yourself.
10. Walk quietly in the halls.

Handy Class Rules

During the first few days of school, lead a discussion encouraging youngsters to think of behaviors that would enable everyone in the class to work well together. As a group, decide what you would like your class rules to be. Emphasize that when everyone does his part to follow the rules, activities in your classroom will be much more fun! Write the rules on a large sheet of paper with the title shown. Next, help each child trace his hand, cut out the shape, and sign his name. Then post the chart on a wall and attach the handprints around it.

Reading motivation • • • • • • • • • • • • • • • Literacy

We Are Readers!

What could make students prouder than showing off their reading skills at the beginning of school? To prepare, cut out a variety of familiar words and phrases from newspapers, magazines, and product wrappers. Display the cutouts and ask volunteers, in turn, to read words that they recognize. Then celebrate youngsters' reading achievement by teaching them the following chant.

One, two, three, four
Readers just walked through the door!
Five, six, seven, eight.
Reading makes us feel just great!
Let's read!

Find reproducible activities on pages 24–29.

Building Friendship

Our names are _____ and _____.

We are friends!

We are alike because _____

_____.

We are different because _____

_____.

_____ says, "If you take a mouse

to _____, he'll ask you for

_____!"

Note to the teacher: Use the top form with "Building Friendship" on page 20.
Use the bottom form with "Eek! A Mouse!" on page 21.

Marvelous Me

1. I can write my name.
   _____

   _ _ _ _ _ _ _ _ _ _ _ _ _

   _____

2. I can write the date.
   _____

   _ _ _ _ _ _ _ _ _ _ _ _ _

   _____

3. I can write numbers.
   _____

   _ _ _ _ _ _ _ _ _ _ _ _ _

   _____

4. I love to _____.
   _____

   _ _ _ _ _ _ _ _ _ _ _ _ _

   _____

5. I am _ _ _ _ _ _ _

   _____

   years old.

6. I can draw myself.

Note to the teacher: Have each child complete this page at various times of the school year. Compile the completed pages to show progress made during the year.

Loading Zone

Name _____

Color the objects with matching letters in each row.

Feel the Beat!

Name _____

Name each picture.

Clap to show the word parts.

✂ Cut. 🖊 Glue to match.

| 1 | 1 | 1 | 2 | 2 | 2 | 3 |

Colorful Crayons

Name _____

✏️ Write.
🖍️ Color.

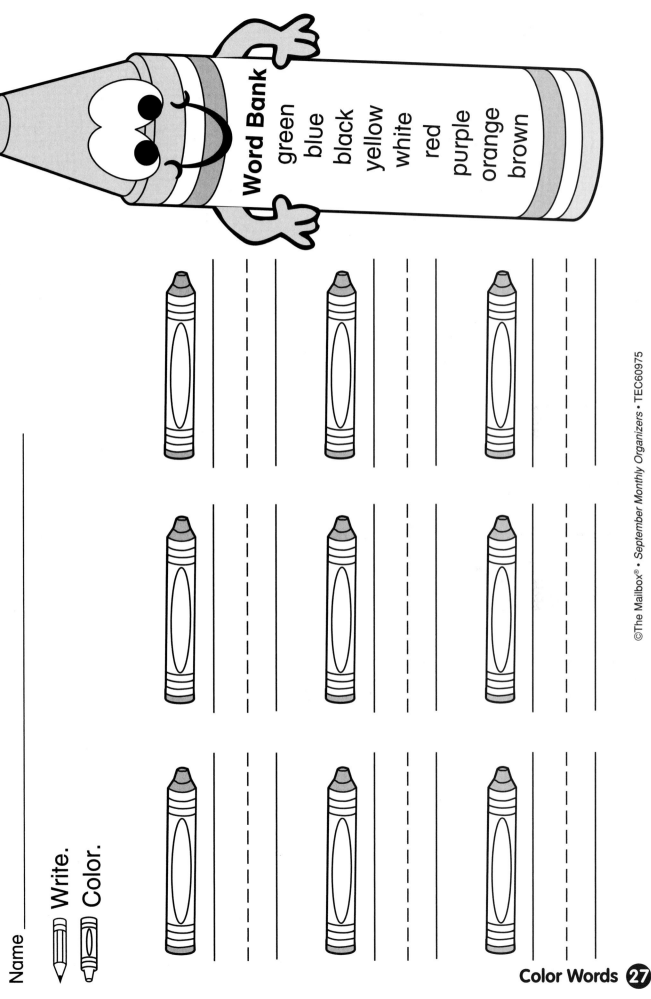

Word Bank

green
blue
black
yellow
white
red
purple
orange
brown

The Name Game

Name _____

My name has eight letters.

✏️ Write the names of four classmates.

1.			
2.			
3.			
4.			

The longest name has _____ letters.

The shortest name has _____ letters.

Is there a letter that is in all the names? _____ What is it? _____

©The Mailbox® • September Monthly Organizers • TEC60975

Snacktime

Name _____

✏ Write the missing numbers.

A.
 **3**       **5**   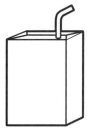    **7** 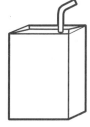

B.
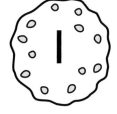 **1**   **2**   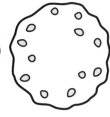   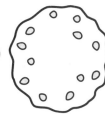 **4**   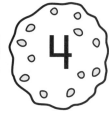    **6**

C.
 **2**       **4**    **5**    

D.
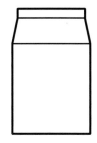    **5**    **6**       **8** 

E.
 **5**       **9** **10**

©The Mailbox® • *September Monthly Organizers* • TEC60975

Number Order to 10 29

Open House

Literacy

Writing

Welcome!

Welcome parents to your classroom with these personalized greetings from their children. Have each child color and cut out a copy of the welcome sign on page 34. Then have him glue the sign to the top of a 12" x 18" sheet of construction paper as shown. Help him write a personal note at the bottom of his paper; then have him sign his name and draw a picture of his family. On the night of open house, place each child's greeting on his desk. As parents arrive, direct them to their personalized greetings and encourage them to showcase these special projects at home.

Classroom contributions

Management

Supply Roundup

This special can of pencils points out classroom needs and encourages parents to contribute. Make several construction paper copies of the pencil patterns on page 33. Label each pencil with a needed classroom supply, such as paper plates or stickers. Cut out the pencils and store them in a can labeled as shown. Then place the can in an open area for easy access. During open house, invite parents who are interested in making classroom contributions to pick a pencil. Each time a donation is received, send a personal note of thanks to the appropriate family.

If desired, also use open house as a time to recruit parent volunteers for classroom help. Simply copy a supply of the form on page 34 and set it beside the pencil can. Then, during your presentation, briefly mention this form too.

Get ready for an impressive open house with these crowd-pleasing ideas.

Input From Parents

Use this simple survey to learn more about your students from the people who know them best—their parents! Before open house begins, place a copy of the survey on page 35 on each child's desk. If possible, ask parents to complete the survey during their visit (or encourage them to take it with them and return it to school the next day). Tell parents you will promptly follow up on any concerns they have with a personal phone call or scheduled meeting. After parents leave, collect any uncompleted surveys. Then label each survey with the appropriate student name, attach a return request, and send it home to parents the following day.

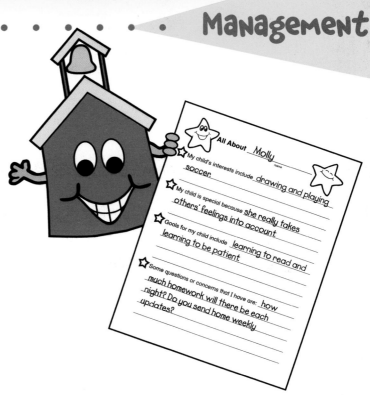

All About __Molly__
name

My child's interests include __drawing and playing soccer.__

My child is special because __she really takes others' feelings into account.__

Goals for my child include __learning to read and learning to be patient.__

Some questions or concerns that I have are: __how much homework will there be each night? Do you send home weekly updates?__

Favorite Subjects

Here's a fun way to encourage open house participation and create a graphing activity. Make two large graphs like the ones shown. On the day of open house, post the graph with the present tense question. Read the question aloud and direct each youngster to answer it by attaching a personalized sticky note to the appropriate row. Later, as parents enter the classroom for open house, ask them to write their names on individual sticky notes and attach them to the other graph. Parents are sure to find the graphs interesting, and students will have fun comparing them the following day!

What IS Your Favorite?

Reading	Janet	Ron	Cindy	Jerry	
Math	Larry	Marge	Paula		
Science	Sandy				

What WAS Your Favorite?

Reading	Doug	Barb	Bob	Tom	Maxine
Math	Don	Sam	Kelly		
Science	Bill	Dave	Emily		

The Question Bag

What learning centers do we have in our class?

How often do we get to check books out of the library?

What's Up?

Use the results of this writing activity at open house to inform parents about classroom activities. To begin, enlist students' help in creating a list of school topics that they think their parents would like to know about. Then, on a slip of paper, help each child write a question about a topic from the list. Collect the slips and place them in a decorated gift bag. During open house, explain to parents that their children wrote questions to give them insight on typical classroom activities. Invite each parent, in turn, to draw a question from the bag and read it aloud for you to answer. After all the questions have been read, invite parents to write any questions they may have and deposit them in the bag. The following day, compile a list of questions and answers and send a copy home to each parent.

Student-Guided Tours

If your school encourages students to attend open house with their parents, then this idea is for you! A few days before the scheduled event, discuss the role of a tour guide. Then have students help create a list of attractions from the classroom and around the school that they would like to show their parents. Use the list to create a tour plan similar to the one shown. On the day of open house, give each child a copy of the plan and review its contents. Ask each child to leave the plan on his desk before leaving for the day. Then, during open house, have each child use the plan to guide his parents to the featured attractions. When each child has finished his tour, place a sticker on his tour plan. The following day, invite students who were not able to attend open house to take home a tour plan and explain each item to their parents.

Open House Tour
1. my desk
2. calendar
3. math center
4. my journal
5. computer lab
6. library

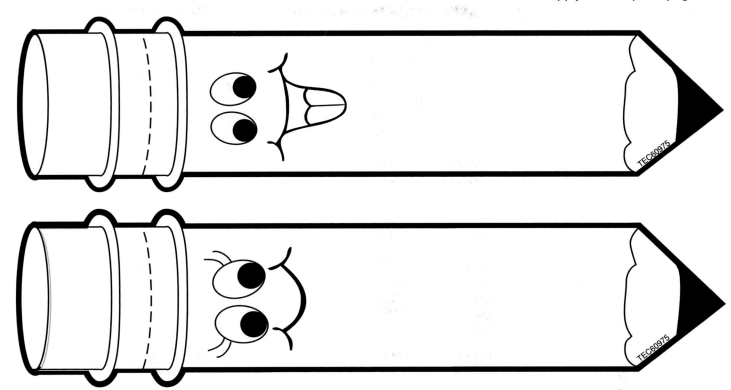

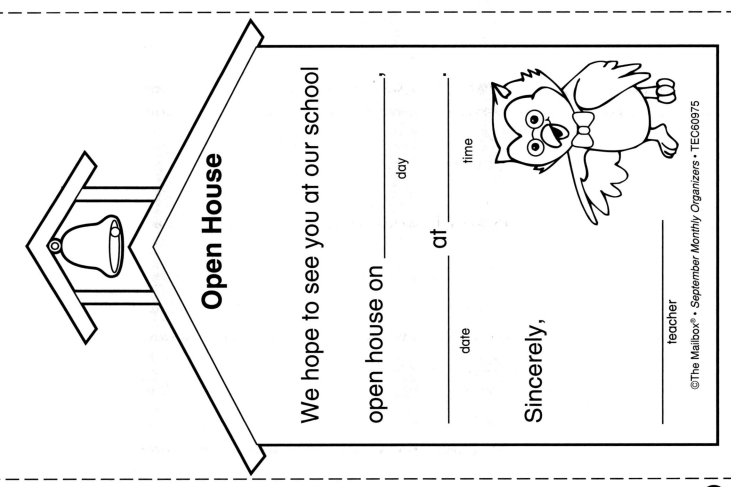

Open House

We hope to see you at our school

open house on _____ ,
                   day

at _____ .
     time

_____
 date

Sincerely,

_____
 teacher

©The Mailbox® • September Monthly Organizers • TEC60975

Note to the teacher: Program the invitation and then make a copy to send home with each child.

©The Mailbox® • *September Monthly Organizers* • TEC60975

Lend Us a Hand!

Please check the areas you would like to help with.

☐ holiday parties

☐ field trips

☐ classroom activities

☐ reading to students

☐ donating supplies

_____   _____
            name   phone number

Thank you for volunteering to help!

©The Mailbox® • *September Monthly Organizers* • TEC60975

Note to the teacher: Use with "Supply Roundup" on page 30.

All About _____
name

⭐ My child's interests include _____

_____

_____

⭐ My child is special because _____

_____

_____

⭐ Goals for my child include _____

_____

_____

⭐ Some questions or concerns that I have are _____

_____

_____

_____

Note to the teacher: Use with "Input From Parents" on page 31.   **Open House** 35

Apples

• • • • • • • • • • • • *Letter identification*

All in a Row

Make five copies of the apple patterns from page 40 on red construction paper and then cut them out. Place ten alphabet cards along your chalk tray and position an apple pattern in front of each one. Lead students in singing the song below and have a child remove an apple at the appropriate time. Pause at the end of the song for youngsters to name the letter. Then remove the letter card and repeat the song until each hidden letter has been identified.

(sung to the tune of "Ten in a Bed")
Oh what do I see?
Some apples in a tree.
Let's pick one; let's pick one.
What's hiding behind it
For us to find?

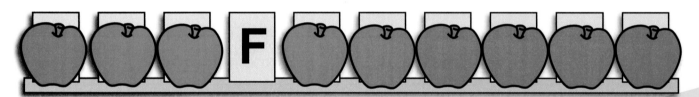

Sort by size or color • • • • • • • • • • • • • **Math**

An "A-peel-ing" Sort

To prepare for this center, trace the apple on page 41 on white paper to make a large apple pattern. Then make several different-colored construction paper copies of this pattern and the apple patterns on page 40. Cut out the apples and store them in a basket at a center. A visiting child can sort the apples in two different ways: by size and by color.

Pick from these apple-themed activities for bushels of learning!

So Many Seeds!

No matter how you slice it, this apple center provides a lot of counting and numeral-matching practice! Use the pattern on page 42 to make a supply of white construction paper apples. If desired, color the outside edge of each apple. Cut out the apples and then use a different puzzle cut to cut each apple in half. Next, program one half of each apple with a numeral and draw the matching number of seeds on the corresponding half. (Or program one half with seeds to form an addition problem and the corresponding half with the answer.) Place the cutouts at a center. A child counts the seeds on an apple half. When she finds the cutout with the corresponding numeral, she places the two cutouts together. She continues in the same manner until all the halves have been matched.

Pass the Apples!

Copy the apple patterns on page 40 on construction paper to make a class supply. Cut out the apples and attach to each one a picture (clip art or sticker) that illustrates a different CVC or CVCe word. Place the apples in a small basket. To begin, have youngsters sit in a circle. While you play recorded music, have students pass the basket around the circle. Every few moments, stop the music and ask the child who is holding the basket to remove an apple and name the picture on it. Then have the class join him in repeating the beginning sound (or letter) of the word. Continue in this manner for several more rounds.

Pick of the Crop

Youngsters recognize their classmates' names with a bumper crop of apples! Use the patterns on page 40 to make a class supply of construction paper apples and leaves. Glue each child's photo to a separate apple and program a leaf with her name. If desired, write the child's name on the back of the apple cutout for self-checking. Then place the apples and leaves at a center. A child chooses an apple, names the classmate pictured, and finds the corresponding leaf. Then she places the leaf on the apple. She continues in this manner until she has matched all the apples and leaves.

Number words one *through ten* · · · · · · · · · · · · · · · · · · **Math**

Wiggle Worms

For this small-group activity make ten tagboard apples using the patterns on page 40. Program each apple with a different number word from *one* to *ten*. Laminate the apples, cut them out, and use a hole puncher to make ten holes in each apple. Next, cut each of 28 chenille stems in half. Fold over the ends of each piece (to avoid sharp edges) and then twist the pieces into worm shapes. Place the worms and apples in separate containers. Invite each child in a small group to choose an apple. Help him read the number word on his apple and count out the corresponding number of worms. Then have him poke each worm into a different hole in his apple. Continue in the same manner until each apple has the correct number of hungry worms!

"Apple-licious"

Place a set of plastic alphabet letters and several copies of page 41 at a table. Gather a small group of students and give each child a copy of the page. Explain that all the items pictured on the apple have apples as an ingredient. Help youngsters identify each picture and read each word. Then have each child choose one item and use plastic letters to form the corresponding word, making sure the child forms the word from left to right. Encourage each child to repeat the activity until he has created each word shown. As an alternate activity, challenge each child to write a sentence that includes one or more of the words.

Science • • • • • • • • • • • • • • • • Names of the seasons

Apple Tree Season

Make a copy of the booklet on pages 42–43 for each child. To begin, read aloud *The Seasons of Arnold's Apple Tree* by Gail Gibbons. Then review the seasonal changes illustrated in the book and point out the words *spring, summer, fall,* and *winter.* Have each child personalize her booklet cover and then color it as desired. Next, have her use crayons to embellish each page to show how the apple tree appears during each season, inviting her to refer to the book illustrations if needed. Have each child cut out her booklet cover and pages. Then help her sequence her pages behind her cover and staple the stack to make a booklet. Invite partners to read their booklets to each other.

Find reproducible activities on pages 44–45.

Apple and Leaf Patterns

Use with "All in a Row" and "An 'A-peel-ing' Sort" on page 36, "Pass the Apples!" on page 37, and "Pick of the Crop" and "Wiggle Worms" on page 38.

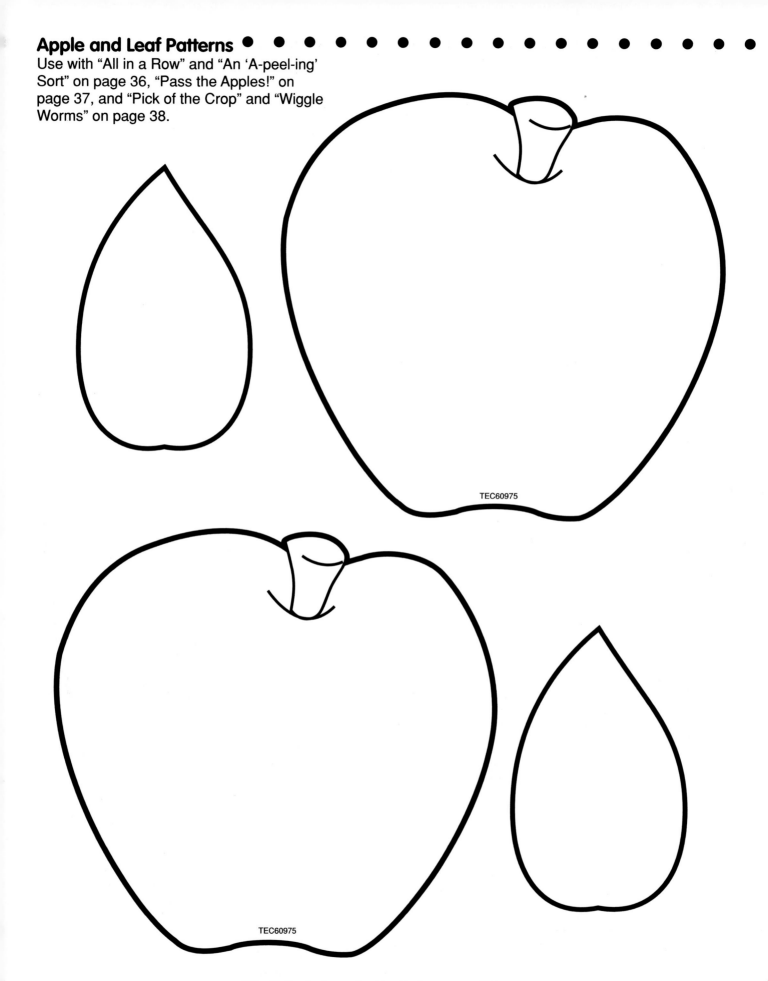

TEC60975

TEC60975

40 Apples

apple

pie

juice

muffin

applesauce

TEC60975

Note to the teacher: Use with "An 'A-peel-ing' Sort" on page 36 and " 'Apple-licious'" on page 39.

Apples 41

Apple Pattern

Use with "So Many Seeds!" on page 37.

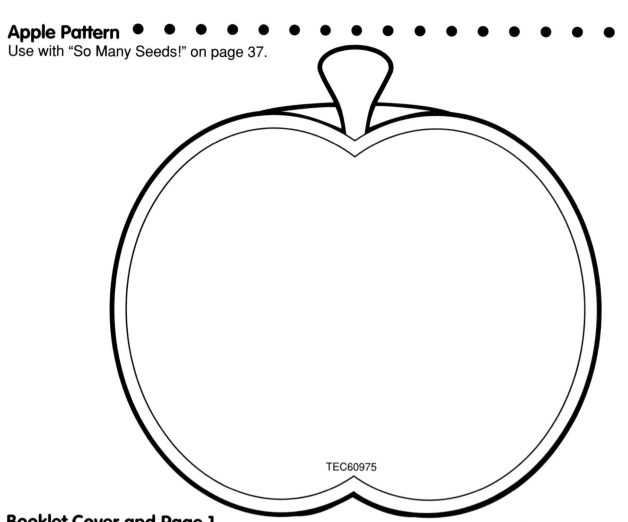

TEC60975

Booklet Cover and Page 1

Use with "Apple Tree Season" on page 39.

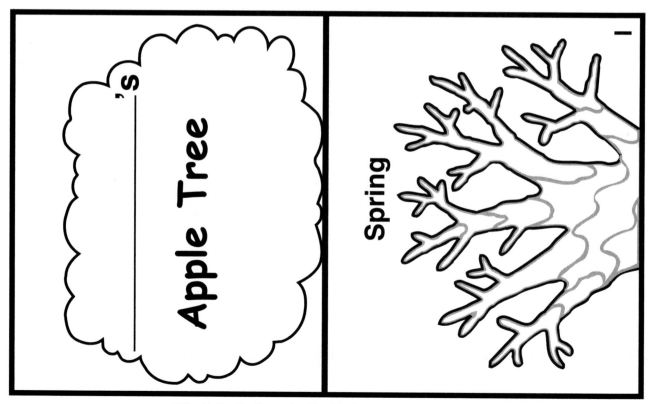

An Armful of Apples

Name _____

✂ Cut.

Glue to match the pictures and the beginning letters.

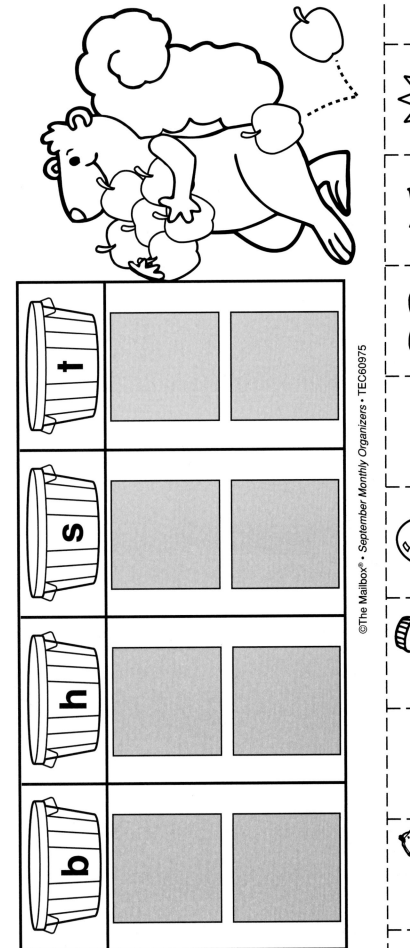

Initial Consonants: b, h, s, t 45

Grandparents

Use the following ideas to spotlight youngsters' grandparents and other older adults on Grandparents Day (annually the first Sunday after Labor Day).

Literacy • • • • • • • • • • • • • • • • • • *Writing*

My grandparent is great at _playing the piano._

by _____ Carter

Wall of Fame

Put your youngsters' writing on display with these cute grandparent creations! Give each child a copy of page 47. Have him color a portrait of his grandparent inside the oval. Then help him complete the sentence starter at the bottom of the page. Invite each child to share his completed project with the class before displaying the projects with the title "Grandparents' Wall of Fame."

Graphing • • • • • • • • • • • • • • • • Math

Graphing Grandparents

We know grandparents are special the whole year through, but what time of year is the most special to them? Find out with this picture-graph activity! In advance, label a graph like the one shown and have each child poll a grandparent to find out which season is his or her favorite. Have each child draw a picture of her grandparent and then label it with her name and her grandparent's name. Post the graph and have each child tape her paper to the appropriate row. Then lead young-sters in a discussion about the graph.

Our Grandparents' Favorite Seasons

Spring	Cassie's Granny	Ted's Pawpaw	Beth's Grandma	
Summer	Alec's Nona	Tony's Granny		
Fall	Sarah's Grandpa	Edward's Popey	Jalen's Nana	Hannah's Granny
Winter	Kevin's Gramps			

Find reproducible activities on pages 48–49.

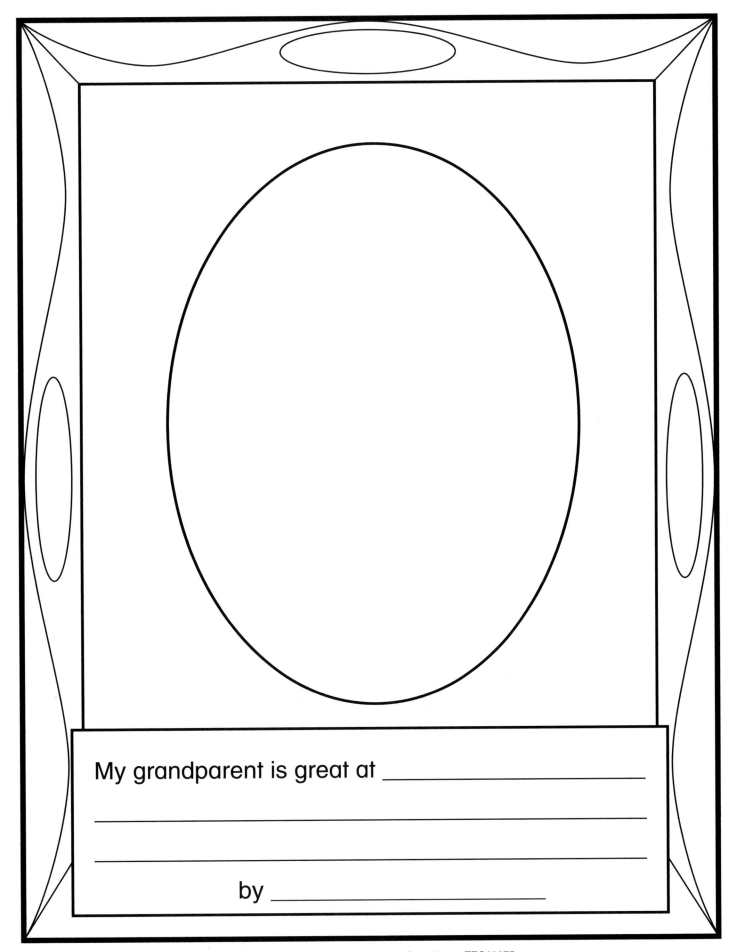

My grandparent is great at _____

_____

_____

by _____

Granny's Goodies

Name _____

Color each set with more.

Grandparents Day Card

Color the pattern to create a picture of you and sign your name. Cut out the pattern and glue a 2" x 12" construction paper strip to each side as shown. Trace your hands on construction paper, cut out the tracings, and glue one hand to the free end of each strip. Accordion-fold each arm to ready the card for delivery!

Here is a hug for you!
Happy Grandparents Day!
Love,

49

Arts & Crafts

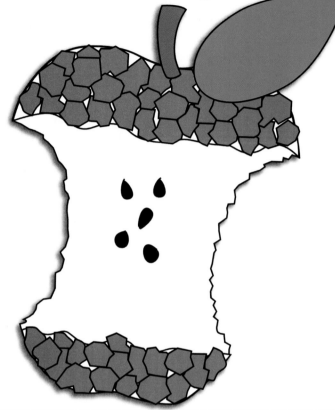

Good to the Core!

To make an apple, cut out a copy of the apple pattern on page 53 along the heavy lines. Tear along the dashed lines to make the apple core. Then tear red construction paper scraps into small pieces. Glue the red pieces to the top and bottom of the apple core. Draw seeds on the center of the core. To complete the project, glue a construction paper stem and leaf to the top.

Happy Birthday!

Help children learn their birthdays while decorating these creative cakes. In advance, label a colorful cake pattern (page 52) for each child with her name and birthday. To complete a cake, a child cuts out the pattern and then uses craft materials such as yarn, ribbon, rickrack, stickers, glitter, and colored glue to decorate the cake. Then she glues an appropriate number of pipe cleaner pieces to the cake for candles.

Sensational Sunflowers

To make a sunflower, cut yellow crepe paper into short lengths and then glue the lengths to the edge of a small paper plate to resemble petals. Dip a pencil eraser in brown tempera paint and make multiple prints in the middle of the flower. After the paint and glue are dry, tape a length of green curling ribbon to the back of the flower for a stem. Finally, hole-punch the top of the flower and attach a yarn hanger. Suspend the flowers from the ceiling to create a sunflower garden in your classroom!

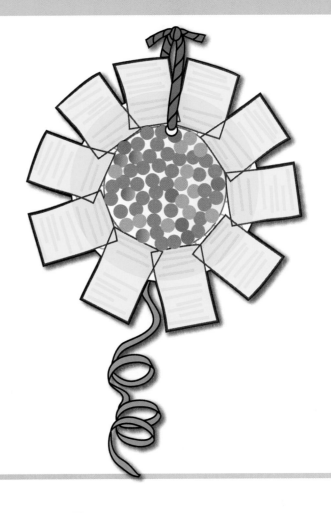

Who's Who?

Students provide the clues for a project that's a must for open house! In advance, create a clue form like the one shown and make a copy for each child. Give each child a skin-toned construction paper oval and have her use arts-and-crafts supplies to create a self-likeness. Next, each child traces her hands on skin-toned construction paper and cuts out the shapes. She then glues the face, the hand cutouts, and a completed copy of the clue form to a 12" x 18" sheet of dark construction paper as shown. Display the completed projects on a wall and encourage youngsters and parents to guess who's who!

I have <u>green</u> eyes.
I have <u>brown</u> hair.
I love to <u>sing</u>.
Who am I?

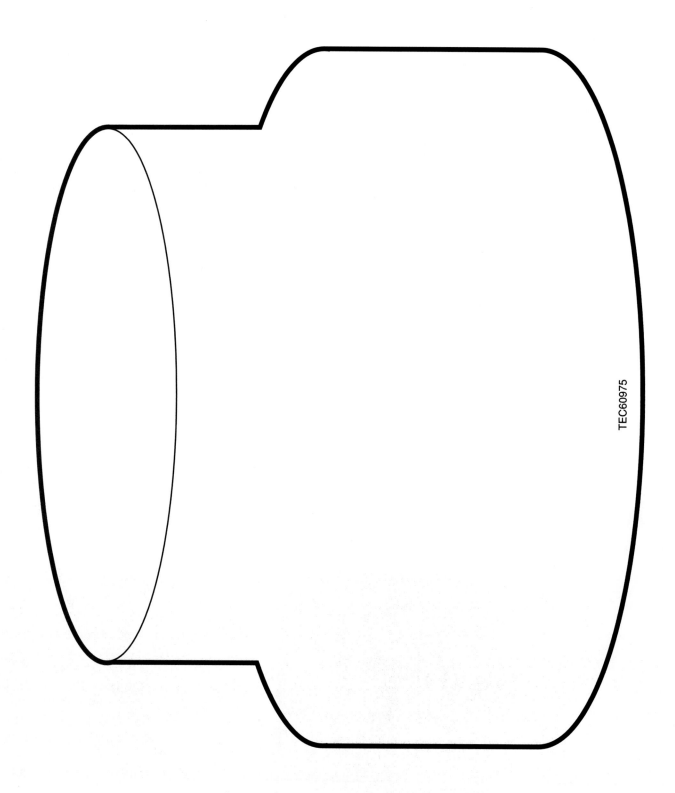

TEC60975

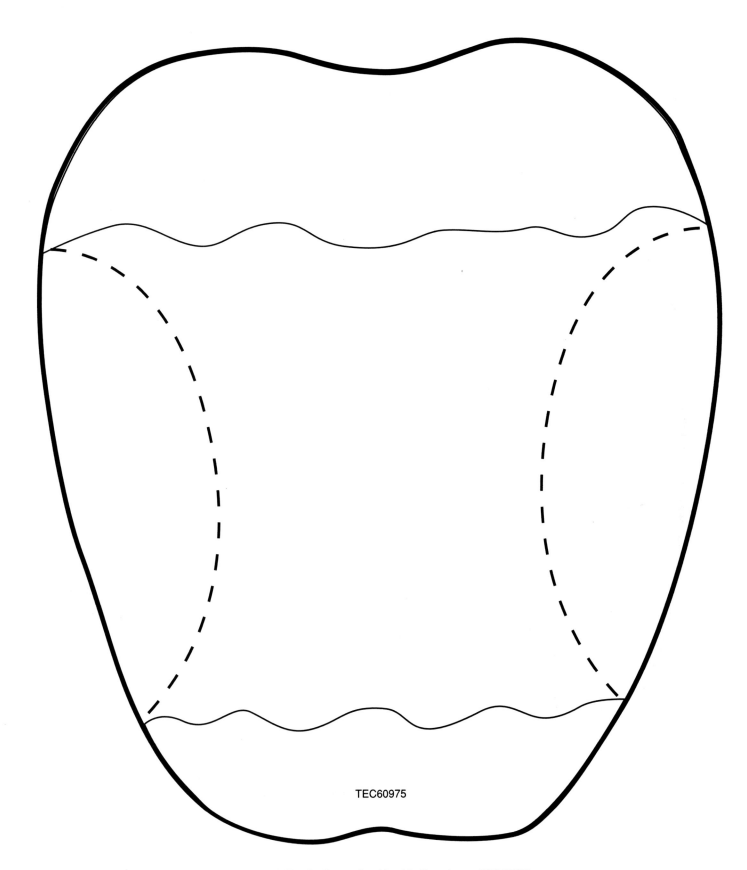

TEC60975

School Bus Safety

Board the bus one at a time.
Keep your feet out of the aisles.
Stay seated.

Face the front of the bus.
Use your quiet voice.
Keep your hands inside
the windows.

Create a large paper school bus, as shown, labeled with a list of bus safety rules. Mount it on a wall and add stuffed-paper wheels and white windows. Give each child a simple head-and-shoulders cutout and have him use crayons and craft materials to decorate it to resemble himself. Each day, display several portraits in the bus windows and review the posted rules.

to add

to use the computer

to subtract

to read big books

It's Time to Learn!

to write my address

to write fun stories

to count to 100

how plants grow

Share with youngsters some of the many things they'll learn this year. Then have each child choose one thing he's looking forward to learning. Help him write this item on a copy of the clock pattern from page 56. Next, instruct him to cut out the clock and hands. Use a brad to attach the hands to the center of each child's clock where indicated. Mount the clocks and the title to complete this timely display.

Displays

"S'more" Great Kids!

Welcome students to your classroom with this tasty-looking bulletin board! Give each child an eight-inch square of white construction paper, a 2" x 8" strip of brown construction paper, and two 1" x 9" strips of tan construction paper. Instruct her to glue the strips to the square as shown to resemble a s'more. Have her write her name on the top graham cracker and draw a self-portrait on the marshmallow section. Mount the completed treats and add the title shown.

Apple of My Eye

The focus of this open house display is the special thoughts shared by students and their families! Post a large paper tree and a basket, on a wall along with the title shown. Give each child a red construction paper copy of the apple pattern on page 57. Have her write or dictate a special message to her family member(s) who will be attending open house; then have her cut it out and add a paper stem and leaf. Attach the apples to the display. During open house, ask parents to jot messages to their children on the cutouts. (Write responses on the apples of those students whose parents were unable to attend.) When school resumes, help each child read her completed apple.

TEC60975

Use with "Apple of My Eye" on page 55.

Dear ________________________,

____

____

Love,

____

Dear ________________________,

____

____

Love,

____

TEC60975

Centers

Literacy ———————————————————————————————— **Names**

Names in Print

With this activity, students practice letter recognition and fine-motor skills at the same time! Supply a center with newspapers, magazines, scissors, glue, construction paper, and assorted art supplies such as yarn, rickrack, crayons, and stickers. A child searches through magazines and newspapers to find the letters in his name. As he finds each letter, he cuts it out and glues it to a sheet of construction paper. When his name is complete, he uses the art supplies to decorate the border of his paper as he likes.

Numerals and sets ———————————————————————— **Math**

School Tools

This game gets youngsters all packed up and ready for school! For each player, you will need a crayon, a pencil, a ruler, scissors, an eraser, a glue stick, a resealable plastic bag, and a copy of the recording sheet on page 60. Place the recording sheets, school tools, and bags at a center along with a die. To play, a child rolls the die and finds the matching number on her recording sheet. Then she places the corresponding school supply in her bag and colors it on her paper. If she already has the item in her bag, play continues with the next child. The game is over when every player has placed each school tool in her bag.

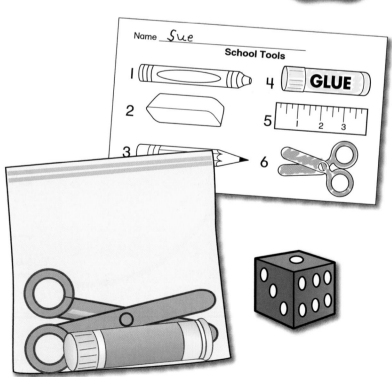

In the Apple Tree

Color and cut out a copy of the tree pattern on page 61. Place the tree, 12 red pom-poms (apples), a die, and scrap paper at a center. To play, a child rolls the die, writes the number on a sheet of paper, and places the corresponding number of apples on her tree. She repeats this process and then adds the numbers on her paper. To check her work, she counts the apples on her tree. She continues play in this manner for a predetermined number of rounds.

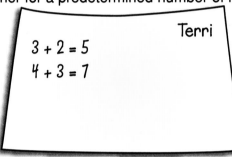

Terri

$3 + 2 = 5$

$4 + 3 = 7$

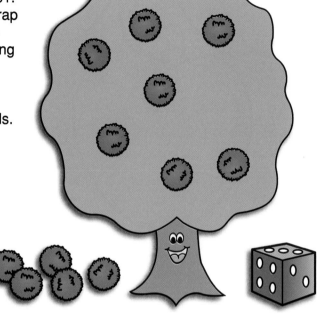

Literacy

Rhyming words

Apple Rhymes

To prepare, color and cut out four copies of the tree pattern on page 61. Also make two red construction paper copies of the apple patterns on page 60 and cut them out. Divide the apples into four sets of three apples each and program each set with rhyming words. Store the apples in a small basket; then place the basket and the trees at a center. A child searches through the apples to find rhyming sets and places each set on a separate tree.

Apple Patterns
Use with "Apple Rhymes" on page 59.

Name _____

School Tools

1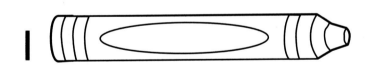

2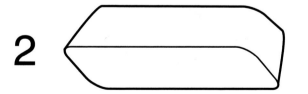

3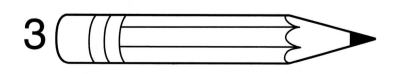

4  **GLUE**

5

6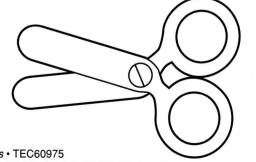

Note to the teacher: Use with "School Tools" on page 58.

Tree Pattern
Use with "Apple Rhymes" and "In the
Apple Tree" on page 59.

TEC60975

Games

Self-esteem

Sunny Smiles

This sunny game teaches youngsters to appreciate themselves and others! Cut out two sun shapes and label one with the word *me* and one with the word *you*. Place the labeled suns in a plastic bucket. To play, sit with youngsters in a circle and pass the bucket to the first child. Have her draw one sun and help her read the word. If the word is *me,* ask her to say something sunny about herself. If the word is *you,* ask her to say something sunny about the child to her left. Then have her put the sun back in the bucket and pass it to the next child. Continue play in this manner until each child has had a turn.

Recognize and order numbers 1–10

Math

Bushels of Fun!

To prepare, die-cut ten red construction paper apples (or make copies of the apple pattern on page 40). Program each apple with a different number from 1 to 10. Next, invite ten student volunteers to stand in a line with their backs to the other students. Mix up the apples; then give each student one apple to hold at chest level with the number facing out. At your signal, have the ten students face their classmates. Call on seated students to help you order the apples from 1 to 10. Repeat the process until each student has had a turn as an apple.

Musical Names

Get youngsters in tune with the sound of classmates' names during this fun group game! In advance, write each child's name on a separate seasonal cutout such as the apple pattern on page 40. Next, invite your group to sit in a circle, and give each child one apple. Then play some lively music and have students quickly pass the apples around the circle. After a few moments, stop the music as a signal for youngsters to stop passing the apples. In turn, help each of several children read aloud the name on the apple he holds. Have him show the apple to the group as he repeats the name. Then start the music again and resume the game.

Barnyard Lotto

For this partner game, give each pair of students two copies of pages 64 and 65 and a supply of game markers. Have each twosome cut out the gameboards and pattern strips and then combine the strips and stack them facedown. To play, Player 1 takes a strip, says the pattern aloud, and extends it by naming the animal that comes next in the pattern. If she has the corresponding animal on her gameboard and it is uncovered, she covers it with a game marker. Then she places her strip in a discard pile. Player 2 takes a turn in a similar manner. Play continues until a child covers three animals in a row.

Barnyard Lotto

©The Mailbox® • September Monthly Organizers • TEC60975

TEC60975

TEC60975

TEC60975

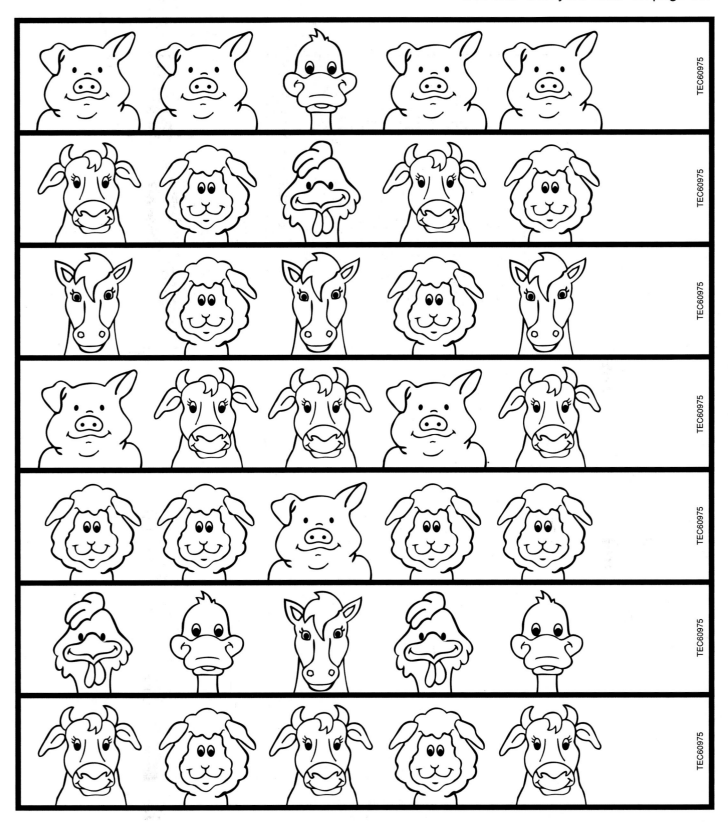

TEC60975
TEC60975
TEC60975
TEC60975
TEC60975
TEC60975
TEC60975

Management Tips

Happy, Happy Birthday!

Prepare for a year of happy birthdays with this timely tip. Before school begins, fill out a class set of birthday cards with your best wishes and signature. Place each card in an envelope. Later, when you receive your class list, add each child's name and birthdate to an envelope. Then organize the envelopes by month and store them with your monthly planning materials.

"Goal-Getters"

Score big with this incentive plan, which has the class setting its own behavior goals! Cut out ten brown construction paper copies of the football pattern on page 67. Also draw a football goal on a bulletin board as shown. Use Sticky-Tac to attach each football along the bottom of the board. With students' help, determine a positive behavior to focus on, such as walking quietly in the halls. Write the goal on a paper strip and attach it above the goalpost. Each time you observe the class exhibiting the featured behavior, attach a football over the goalpost. When all the footballs have been "kicked" over the post, reward the class with a special treat or privilege.

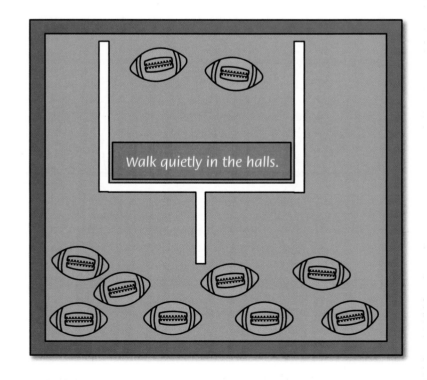

Football Pattern

Use with "'Goal-Getters'" on page 66.

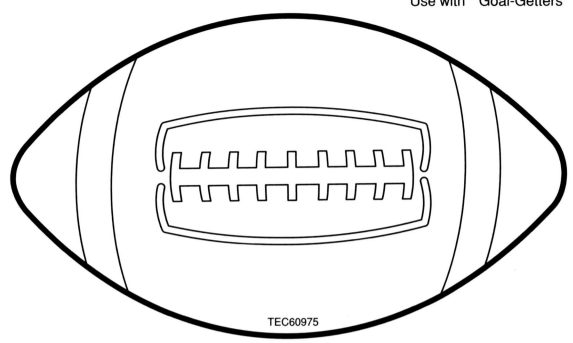

TEC60975

Good Apple Awards

Make a supply of red, yellow, and green construction paper awards to reward students' positive behavior.

LOOK WHO'S A

GOOD APPLE!

TEC60975

YOU ARE A

GOOD APPLE!

TEC60975

CONGRATULATIONS!

YOU ARE A GOOD APPLE!

TEC60975

GOOD APPLE AWARD

TEC60975

SMILE!

YOU ARE A GOOD APPLE!

TEC60975

THANKS FOR BEING A GOOD APPLE!

TEC60975

Time Fillers

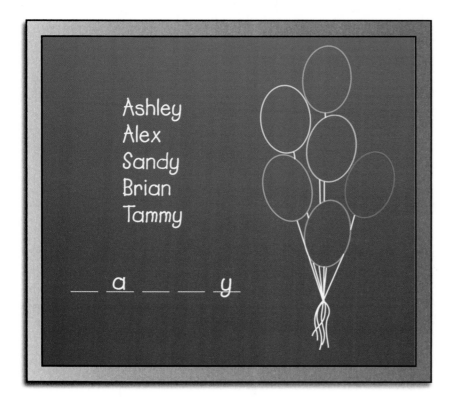

The Name Game

Youngsters practice recognizing and spelling their classmates' names with this high-flying activity! On the board, write the names of a few students and draw a few balloons. Secretly choose one name. Then draw one blank to represent each letter in the name. Invite students to take turns guessing the letters in the name. Write each correct guess on the corresponding line. Each time an incorrect letter is named, "pop" one balloon by erasing it. Continue in this manner until the name is guessed or all the balloons have been "popped."

On-a-Roll Review

Roll through the school year with this thrifty review idea! Recycle extra reproducible skill sheets by cutting apart the individual problems (or questions) from each sheet. Then place the problems in a colorful plastic container. Whenever you have a few extra minutes, ask a child to choose one problem from the container. Help her read the problem to the class. Then encourage students to answer as quickly as possible.

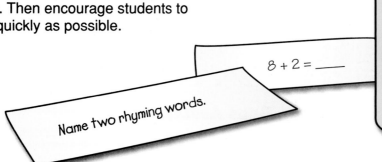

Apple of Your Eye!

Use spare minutes to boost youngsters' self-esteem! At the beginning of the year, write each child's name on an individual apple cutout (pattern on page 40). Then place the apples in a basket. When you have extra time, draw one apple from the basket. This person becomes the Apple of Your Eye and stands. Invite the featured child's classmates to ask her two or three questions about her favorite hobbies, foods, sports, etc. What a great way to make each child feel special *and* help youngsters get acquainted with their new classmates!

Wow! Anna's the apple of my eye!

Anna

I am a good soccer player.

Wiggle and Share

Encourage friendships *and* get the wiggles out with this movement activity. Invite youngsters to dance and wiggle around an open area of the classroom. After a few moments, signal for them to stop. Then have each child turn to the nearest classmate and tell him one special thing. (Consider asking students to share their favorite hobbies, fun summer memories, or what they usually do after school.) After providing a few minutes for students to share, give a signal for them to resume wiggling and repeat the activity.

Journal Prompts

- It's back-to-school time! What do you want to learn this year? Why?

- Do you think you would be a good teacher? Why?

- Grandparents Day is in September. What things do you like to do with your grandparents or senior friends?

- Do you think an apple would taste better if it were a different color, like blue or purple? Why?

- Johnny Appleseed loved plants and animals. What things in nature do you like? Why?

- Write a sample lunch menu for the school cafeteria.

- Why is it important to follow the rules when riding the bus?

Use one or more of the following ideas and the bus pattern on page 72 to get your youngsters on board with writing.

- Give each child a copy of the pattern and have her draw a picture of herself in the bus. Then help her write two or three things about herself on the side of the bus.

- Use the bus pattern for journal writing. Copy the last prompt from above onto a copy of the bus pattern and add writing lines if desired; then make a class supply.

- Going on a field trip? After the trip, give each child a copy of the bus pattern and have him write about the experience.

Picture It!

For this caption-writing activity, take a photograph of each child engaged in a classroom activity. Give each child his photo and a copy of one of the frame patterns on page 73. Have him color and cut out the frame and then glue the photo to it. On a paper strip, instruct him to write a sentence telling what is happening in the photo. Then have him glue the frame and the paper strip to a sheet of colorful construction paper. Bind the completed pages between covers and add the title "Hard at Work in Our Classroom!"

I like to read about cars.

Farm Scene Story Starter

To create the background for a farm scene, cover the top portion of a bulletin board with blue paper and the bottom portion with green paper. Have each student use arts-and-crafts materials to make a cutout of a person, an animal, or an object found on a farm. Add the cutouts to the display.

Next, have students brainstorm story topics related to the scene. Each day, develop a chosen topic into a class story on chart paper. Post the completed stories near the display and reread them periodically during storytime.

A Weird Day
One day the rooster at Old MacDonald's farm slept late. None of the animals knew when to get up!

Bus Pattern

Use with the ideas at the bottom of page 70.

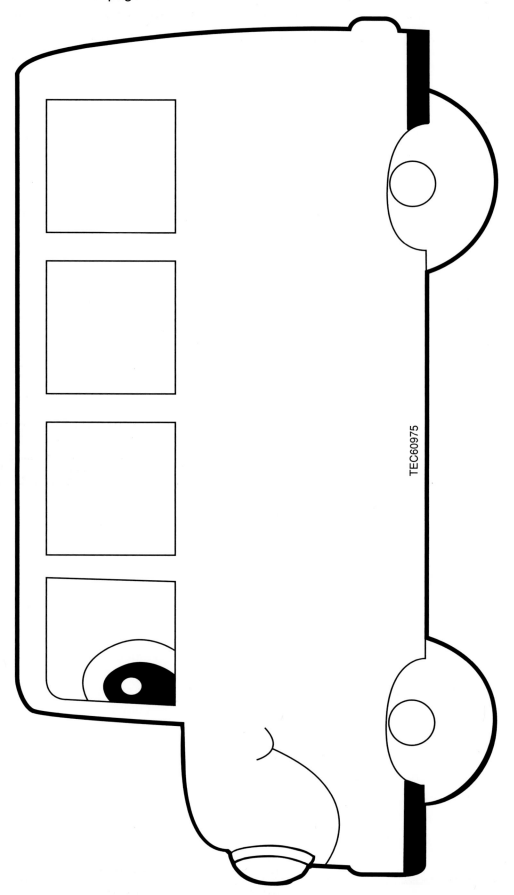

©The Mailbox® • *September Monthly Organizers* • TEC60975

©The Mailbox® • *September Monthly Organizers* • TEC60975

Cool Counters

A ready-to-use center mat and cards

Matching sets to numerals and number words

Materials:
center mat to the right
center cards on pages 77 and 79
2 resealable plastic bags

Preparing the center:
Cut out the cards and select ones to make the best skill review for your youngsters. Store the remaining cards for later use. Cover the third center direction as needed.

Using the center:
1. A child removes the cards from the bag and lays them faceup in the center area.
2. She puts a numeral card on the center.
3. She places a matching number of seed cards on the apple. (If appropriate, she also places the matching word card on the center.)
4. To check her work, she turns over the numeral card (and word card). If the same number of seeds are on the card(s) and the apple, her work is complete. If not, she continues her work until she makes a match.
5. She repeats Steps 2 through 4 for each remaining numeral card.

Follow-Up
After a student completes the center activity for number words through five, use the skill sheet on page 81 for more practice.

Cool Counters

Put ▢.
Count 🌰 to match.
Put ▢.
Check.

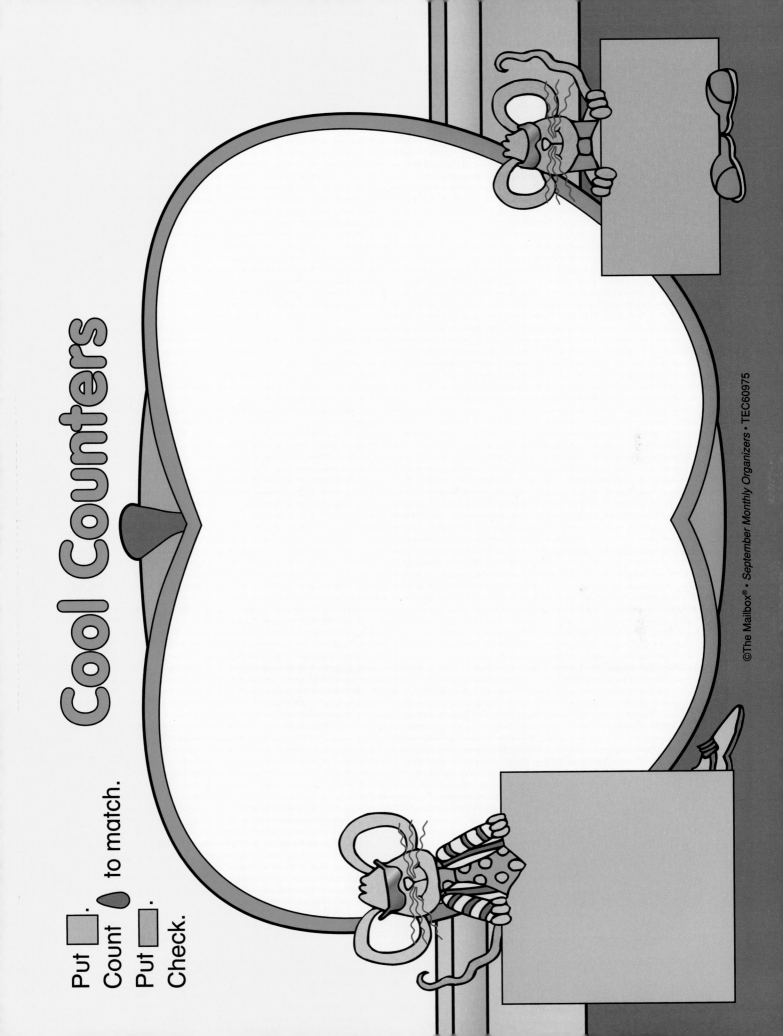

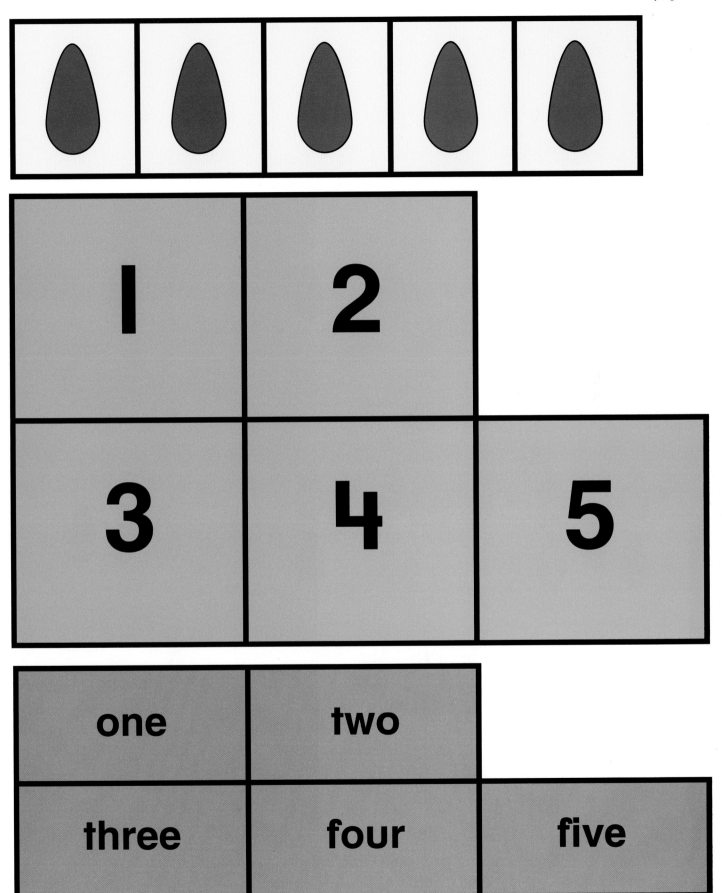

Cool
Counters
TEC60975

Cool
Counters
TEC60975

Cool
Counters
TEC60975

Cool
Counters
TEC60975

Cool
Counters
TEC60975

Cool Counters
TEC60975

Cool Counters
TEC60975

Cool Counters
TEC60975

Cool Counters
TEC60975

Cool Counters
TEC60975

Cool Counters
TEC60975

Cool Counters
TEC60975

Cool Counters
TEC60975

Cool Counters
TEC60975

Cool Counters
TEC60975

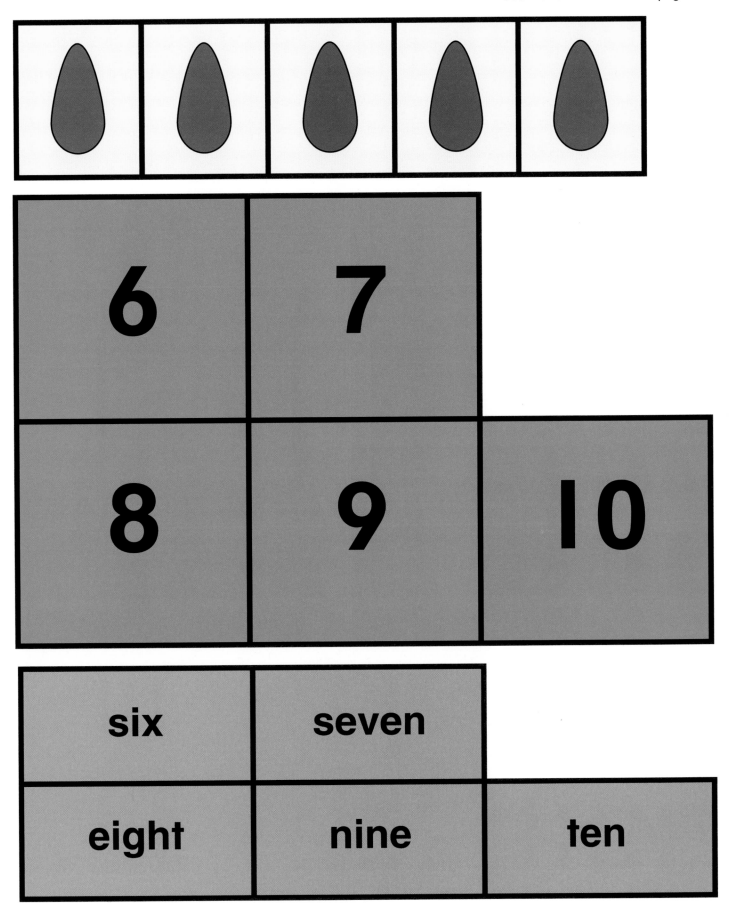

6	7	
8	9	10

six	seven	
eight	nine	ten

Cool
Counters
TEC60975

Cool
Counters
TEC60975

Cool
Counters
TEC60975

Cool
Counters
TEC60975

Cool
Counters
TEC60975

Cool Counters
TEC60975

Cool Counters
TEC60975

Cool Counters
TEC60975

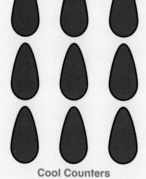

Cool Counters
TEC60975

Cool Counters
TEC60975

Cool Counters
TEC60975

Cool Counters
TEC60975

Cool Counters
TEC60975

Cool Counters
TEC60975

Cool Counters
TEC60975

80 Cool Counters

Yum, Yum, Yum!

Name _____

🖍 Draw 🥜s.

✂️ Cut.

🧴 Glue.

2

1

5

4

3

4

2

| one | two | two | three | four | four | five |

Gus Got on the Bus!

A ready-to-use center mat and cards for two different learning levels

Materials:

center mat to the right
picture cards on page 85
picture word cards on page 87
2 resealable plastic bags

Preparing the centers:

Cut out the cards and place each color-coded set in a separate bag.

Using the centers:

1. A child removes the cards from one bag and lays them faceup in the center area.
2. He names the picture (or word) on each smaller card before he places it on the mat.
3. He names the picture on a larger card and places it below the card whose picture names a rhyme.
4. He repeats Step 3 until every card is placed.
5. To check his work, he turns over each group of cards. If the colors match, he removes the cards. If not, he turns the cards over and rearranges them until they are sorted correctly.

Follow-Up

After a child completes a center activity, use the skill sheet on page 89 for more practice.

Gus Got on the Bus!

Say and put ☐.
Say and sort ☐.
Check.

SCHOOL BUS

Woof!

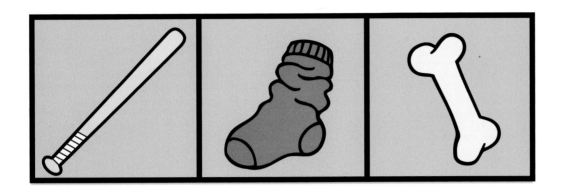

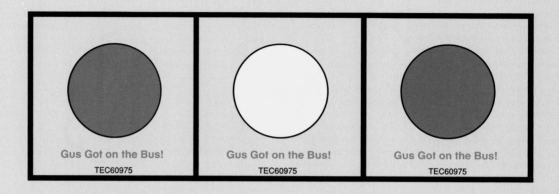

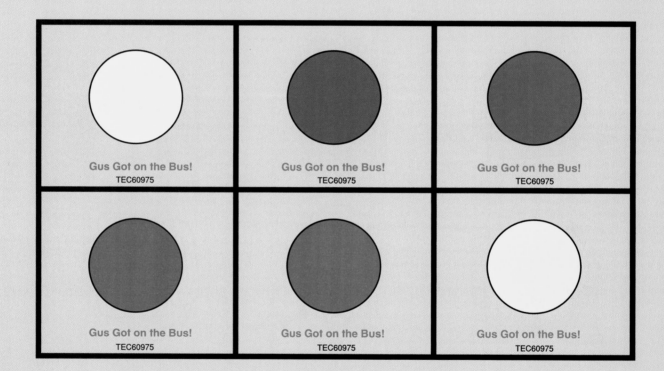

chest   ice   plug

nest   vest   dice

mice   mug   rug

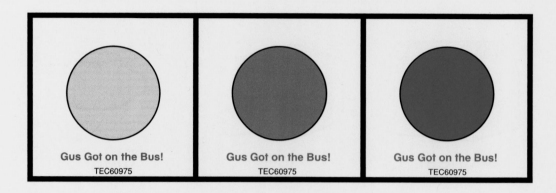

Gus Got on the Bus!
TEC60975

Gus Got on the Bus!
TEC60975

Gus Got on the Bus!
TEC60975

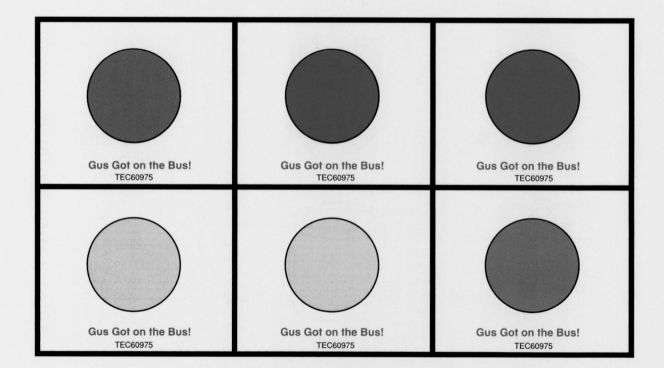

Gus Got on the Bus!
TEC60975

Gus Got on the Bus!
TEC60975

Gus Got on the Bus!
TEC60975

Gus Got on the Bus!
TEC60975

Gus Got on the Bus!
TEC60975

Gus Got on the Bus!
TEC60975

Gus on the Bus

Name _____

Find the rhymes.

✂ Cut.

🧴 Glue.

● Time to Rhyme

Name _____

Name each picture.

Color the rhymes.

©The Mailbox® • September Monthly Organizers • TEC60975

Rhyming

Game Time!

Cut.

Glue the pictures that begin with **f.**

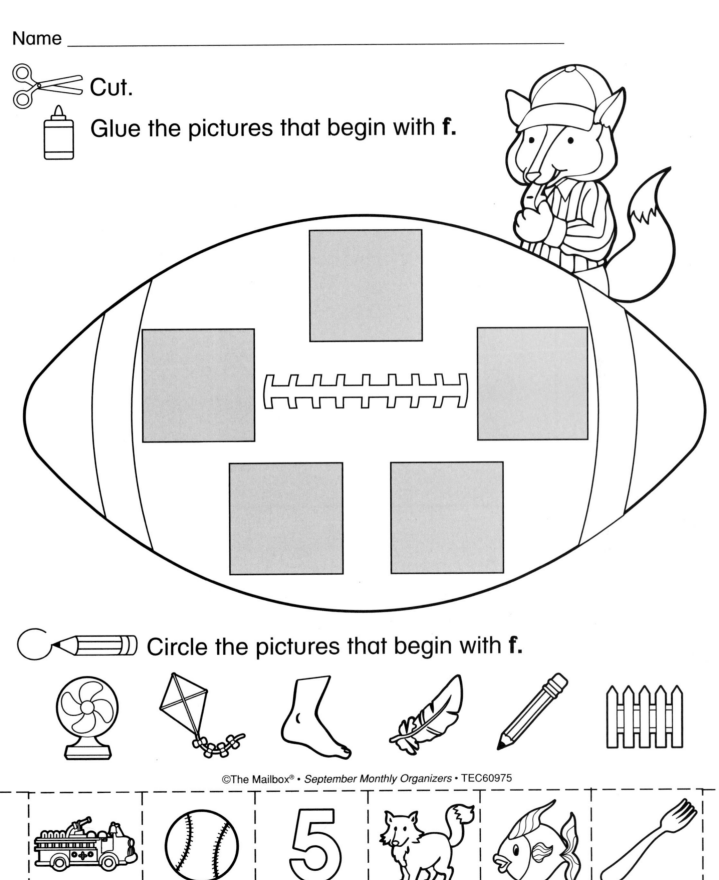

Circle the pictures that begin with **f.**

•••• Off to School •••••••••••••

Name _____

Color the pictures that match the beginning sounds.

m 	    
l 	   
s 	  

Initial Consonants: *l, m, s*

An Apple Orchard

Name _____

Count. Write.
Cut. Glue.

| six | one | four | two | five | three |

One in Each Stall

Name _____

Color. Cut.

Glue one horse in each stall.

Is the number of horses the same as the number of stalls?   Yes   or   No

94

One-to-One Correspondence

School Tools

Name _____

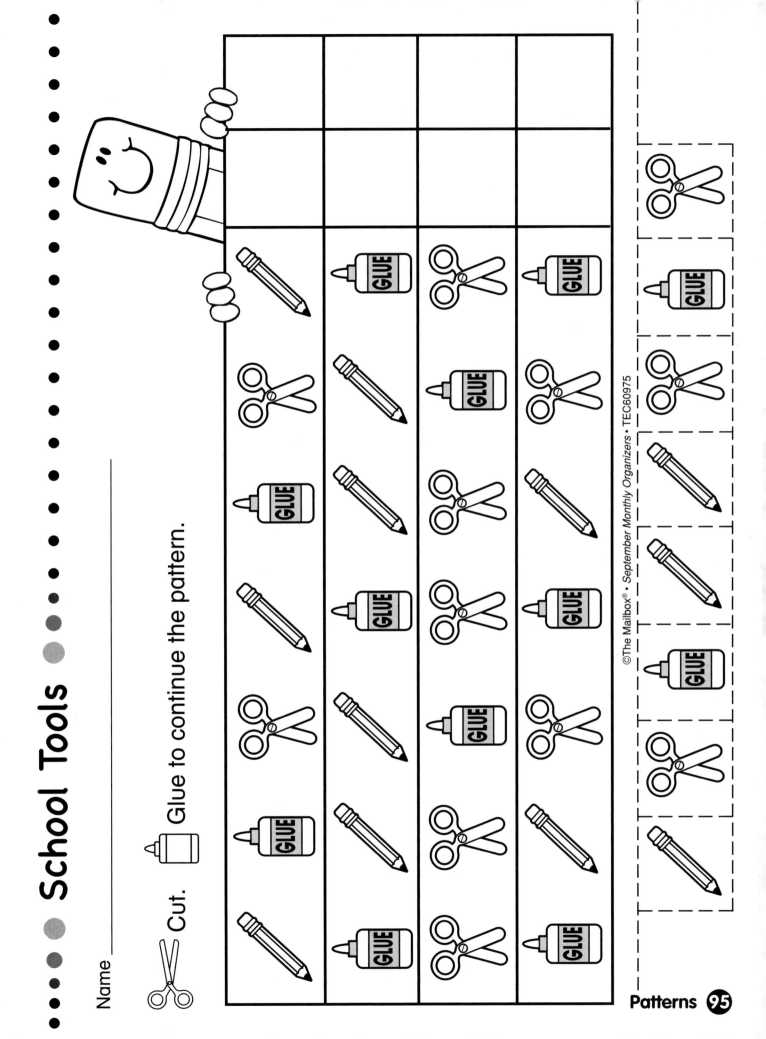

Cut. Glue to continue the pattern.

©The Mailbox® • September Monthly Organizers • TEC60975

Those Are "Sum" Apples!

Name _____

Cut. Add.

Use the apples to help you.

1 + 4 = _____   3 + 2 = _____

2 + 2 = _____   1 + 1 = _____

2 + 1 = _____   4 + 1 = _____

1 + 3 = _____   2 + 3 = _____

Organize Now!™
Grades K–1

Organize in a snap for every new month in the school year using the Monthly Organize Now! series from The Mailbox® Books. Take a look at the guide below to see the popular themes featured in each book of this must-have series.

January	**February**	**March**
TEC60979	TEC60980	TEC60981
New Year	Valentine's Day	Spring
Martin Luther King Jr.	Presidents' Day	St. Patrick's Day
Winter	Dental Health	Rainbows
Polar Animals	Groundhog Day	Wind

April	**May**	**September**
TEC60982	TEC60983	TEC60975
Eggs	Cinco de Mayo	Back-to-School
Rain	Flowers	Apples
Bunnies	Bees	Open House
Pond	Mother's Day	Grandparents
	End of the Year	

October	**November**	**December**
TEC60976	TEC60977	TEC60978
Fall	Thanksgiving	Christmas
Pumpkins	Turkeys	Kindness
Spiders	Families	Hanukkah
Fire Safety	Children's Book Week	Kwanzaa

Monthly Organizing Tools

Ready-to-Go Learning Centers and Skills Practice

This Month in the Classroom

Essential Skills Practice

grades
K-1

Organize SEPTEMBER Now!™

The MAILBOX®

TEC60975

When you're ready to plan September in your classroom, there's only one resource you need: *Organize September Now!*™ Part of The Mailbox® Monthly Organize Now!™ series, this book has everything you need for a successful September:

- **MONTHLY ORGANIZING TOOLS**
  Manage your time, classroom, and students with monthly organizational tools such as calendars, class newsletters, a journal cover, a class list, and clip art.

- **ESSENTIAL SKILLS PRACTICE**
  Practice essential skills this month with engaging activities and reproducibles on themes such as back-to-school, apples, and grandparents.

- **SEPTEMBER IN THE CLASSROOM**
  Carry your monthly themes into every corner of the classroom with arts-and-crafts ideas, bulletin boards and displays, center ideas, games, and much more.

- **READY-TO-GO LEARNING CENTERS AND SKILLS PRACTICE**
  Bring September to life right now with two colorful learning centers and reproducible activities that are ready to use.

Get organized and get ready for a successful month of learning with *Org

Titles in The Mailbox® Monthly Organize Now! series:

TEC60975. Organize September Now!
TEC60976. Organize October Now!
TEC60977. Organize November Now!
TEC60978. Organize December Now!
TEC60979. Organize January Now!
TEC60980. Organize February Now!
TEC60981. Organize March Now!
TEC60982. Organize April Now!
TEC60983. Organize May Now!

ISBN-13: 978-156234668-3
ISBN-10: 156234668-7

14.95

www.themailbox.com

9 781562 346683